KEEP OUT!

BEARS ABOUT!

NO ENTRY!

Sally Grindley and Peter Utton

Hodder
Children's
Books

A division of Hachette Children's Books

The sign says 'Keep Out'.
I think we ought to go back, don't you?

There's another sign saying
'Bears About!'.
Aren't you scared? I am!
I don't want to meet a bear!

BEARS
ABOUT!

Don't tell me
you want to go
through here!

I saw something moving in the grass, did you?
It's gone behind that log.

And what's behind that stone?
I can see a leg sticking out.

I'm not enjoying this.
Can't we go back?

I'm sure we're being watched.
What's up in that tree? Bears can climb trees.

And I don't like the look of that pond. Do you think there are bears hiding under the leaves?

Don't tell me you want to cross that bridge!
There might be bears on the other side!

You'll have to say 'please' very nicely
if you want me to carry on.

What do you think
is behind that wall?

You can peep through
the door if you must,
but we are NOT
going inside!

CHILDREN
WILL BE
EATEN!

DANGER!

KEEP
OUT!

Are you always so naughty?

Whose garden do you think this is?
I hope there aren't any bears in here.

That's someone's house.
We certainly can't go in there!

Look, the front door's open.
Let's go back before someone
catches us here.

Don't tell me you want to go in!

Shhh! Be quiet in case someone hears us.
I wonder who lives here... I hope it's not a bear.

Just don't ask me to go
upstairs, because we're
NOT going to!

Shhh! There's a baby bear
in one of those beds! I said we
shouldn't come upstairs!

Let's creep out quietly
before it wakes up.

Look at those bowls of porridge.
Someone will be coming to eat them! We should go.

Don't tell me you want
to see who's behind that door!

Oh no! It's Daddy Bear and he's coming to get us!

Quick, let's get out of here!